Other books by Patricia Gosling:

A Curious Eye (2006)
Loving and Loss (2009)
A Time of Transition (2011)
Fatal Flaws (2014)
Enduring (2014)
The Long perspective (2015)

The cover picture is of Swansea Bay
seen from the Mumbles Head.

Loving and Leaving

Patricia Gosling
Collected poems

The White Hart

© Patricia Gosling 2018

Patricia Gosling has asserted her right under
the Copyright, Designs and Patents Act 1988
to be identified as the author of this work

All rights reserved

No part of this publication may be reproduced, stored in a
retrieval system, or transmitted in any form or by any
means, electronic, mechanical, photocopying.
recording or otherwise without the prior permission of
the copyright owner.

Published by
White Hart Books
Rode, England
hart@gosmob.eu

To my close companions on the journey
and
for William, who stayed alongside.

Contents

Introduction	*1*

Being
Vignettes	*4*
Post-Christmas Storm	*5*
Autumn Song	*6*
Homing	*7*
Haytime Ditty	*9*
Time Slip	*10*
Melancholy	*11*
Nocturne	*12*
Advent	*13*
Pollen-fever	*14*

Learning
Kick the dog day	*16*
Transference	*18*
Return	*19*
Courtship Dance	*20*
Adolescent Lacuna	*21*
May Song	*22*
A Small Death and Resurrection	*23*
Thankfulness	*25*
Boiling-point	*26*
Episode	*28*
Lesson Learned	*30*

Loss
Grandfather	*32*
Empty Chairs	*34*
Epitaph for Lal	*35*
Manic Mourning	*36*
Gwladys	*37*
Max	*38*

Our Daughter Died
Elegy — 40
Melanie's Death — 41
Regret — 42
Clearing-Out — 43
Bereavement Aftermath — 44
Secrets — 45

Gwalia
Seascape — 48
The Strand, Swansea — 49
St. Non's Bay — 50
Spring Holiday In Pembrokeshire — 51
Hiraeth — 52
Cefn Bryn — 53
Bank Holiday — 54
A timeless moment — 55
Contentment — 56

The Wheel Turns
Aubade — 58
A parent's tale — 59
Cousins — 61
Graduation Day — 62
Josh at eighteen — 63
Easter — 64
Lunch at Oxwich Bay — 65
Time moves on — 67

Blue Devilled
Grief — 70
Christmas blues — 71
Having it all — 72
Denial — 74
Old Age — 76
Cry from the heart — 78
Ending — 80
A magic house — 81

Growing up

Growing up	*84*
Mother	*85*
Betrayal	*87*
Roots	*88*

Relationships

Celebration	*90*
Husband	*91*
Son	*93*
Conference	*95*
Mourning	*97*
Ann	*99*
For Mary	*101*
Insight	*103*
Kathryn	*105*
Birthday Gathering at Nunney	*107*
Women's Lot	*108*

Universals

To the Hospital	*112*
Christmas Story	*113*
Proclamation	*115*
Holding hands	*117*
Mappa mundi	*119*
The search	*120*
Stained glass windows	*121*
Change	*122*
Healing	*124*
Hymn	*125*

Epilogue

Dorothy	*128*
Gifts	*130*
Shifting Sands	*132*
Letting Go	*133*
Clouds	*134*

Notes

	135

Introduction

It is no coincidence that these poems began to be written in the year in which I went into analysis with Martin Miller in Hampstead as part of my training as a psychotherapist. They each emerged with a powerful emotional thrust, out of the blue, or more accurately from the depths of my unconscious, and they arrived fully formed. I rarely made any subsequent amendments. An earlier generation would have said that my muse had visited me.

I am aware of certain themes which recur, in particular that of loss, and also my love of the landscape. Loss became a dominant theme in my life - a ground bass - at the age of 12 months. After that I ceased to be a willing participant in life and became an observer. The natural world became the safe place. It is as if it is only on the death of a significant figure that I know how important they have been to me.
I had forgotten how much I appreciated the landscape on the edge of Bath when we lived in Weston for some years. Daily dog-walking ensured my involvement with it. But my greatest love has been for the Gower peninsula and the sea-coast of Swansea where we lived for sixteen years and later had our holiday home.

I have been surprised how sharply these poems recall for me the times when they were written, as if they each encapsulated something essential of my inner world. Whether the end result is of any interest to anyone else only the reader can say. Looking back, these writings represent the interior life with an honesty which could rarely be expressed by the public persona.

Being

Vignettes

Dark, stark tree trunks soar from a copper floor of fallen
    leaves.
Grey cobbled cottage with its red pan-tiled roof.
Grey-beige woman with her pink-tan corded coat.
Copper-framed mirror with its studded turquoise gems.

I wish I could paint!

[1]

Post-Christmas Storm

The night's shrieking storm has stilled.
The magpies circle their nest on the tallest fir.
The gable ends shine golden through the willow's bare
    branches.
Ranks of bright shields salute the dead king under the hill.

The low road was impassable last night, says my son,
The river meadows a lake, the weir lost under a twelve foot
    rise.
Only a few more inches and the banks will burst.

I roll the sodden newspapers from under the door.
The wild birds whoop with joy at the prospect of breakfast.
I set the duck soup to simmer on the stove.

[2]

Autumn Song

The valley gleams golden through the smoky mist.
The leaves are shades of amber,
Russet, tan and apricot, yallery-green and paper brown.
The colours sing and shimmer, mingle and soothe,
Like the rippling notes of the Chopin Berceuse.

The rooks flap slowly, heavily over the hedge tops;
Low-level flying today.
The gulls, disturbed, shoot skywards,
The season's first horde come a-viking up the river.

I race across the landscape and lower my car window,
Feel the vibrant ionic air across my cheek.
The day is full of joy, and I too am a bird.

Homing

It is a fine day.
I tramp down the motor-way, the traffic mercifully thin.
Before me spreads the open countryside, and the call of
 home.

Once this road spelled excitement, stimulation, freedom.
No more!
Behind me lies London, traffic and anxiety,
Analysis, supervisors, and anxiety,
Fellow-students, rivalry and anxiety,
Examinations, tension and anxiety.
I would be done with the lot of it!

It is a fine day as I turn into the close.
What, no barking! Where's my dog then?
Ah, now I see that rhythmic tail behind the frosted door.
How does he know my particular four-stroke from the others
 passing by?
A flying tumble of multitudinous legs,
A flurry of wet kisses,
An adoration of soft brown eyes.
I am home!

It is a fine day. Let's go for a walk then!
The pasture is sodden under-foot, a cattle-trod mire,
    Farmed as these fields the past a thousand years
The grass lies limp in lank and bleached-bone hanks,
The sloe a dark tracery against the misty valley backdrop.
Only the ivy is green.

The rooks caw their raucous, melancholy, fish-wives gossip,
Circling their tree-top nests,
Revelling in the unexpected winter sun.
The cattle fodder streaks the top field
Like detritus at the close of market day.
We walk along the grey stone, dry-stone wall.
I am content.

[3]

Haytime Ditty

The fields are streaked a ketchup red with sorrel,
The clover and cow-parsley,
The buttercup and bugle,
All nestle in the long, soon-to-be-mown grass.

My love has the gift of eloquence,
His silver tongue weaves spells around his dutiful, surprised
    audience of solid burghers.
He seizes the rapt attention of the too-well dined, too-well
    wined gathering
Of solid, jolly engineers on a night out.
He quells a riot of students, out-talks a conclave of
    academics,
Captures the ear of tycoon and politician.
He whispers sweet nothings in my ear when I am sad and
    need persuasion.

But sometime, just sometimes,
I wish he could be silent.
I should like to hear the song of the skylark,
Watch the swifts weave and dive after the evening gnats.

Time Slip

Skirting the edge of the farm, the edge of the combe,
We tread the path the Roman legions trod,
As they scorned their Celtic brethren in the valleys.
We watch the low sun sink behind the sacred grove.

Time is another dimension here.
We stand on the edge of the world.

[4]

Melancholy

The bull's head blasted oak glowers in the sodden landscape,
Its many twisted horns entwined with ivy.
The autumn morning light has a sullen glow.
The skeletal seed heads of the hedgerow angelica
Sway gauntly in the breeze.

My love is six miles up and heading for the sun,
And I am left behind
To pack away the summer clothes.

[5]

Nocturne

The lights of the town shine clear and bright,
But a soft mist veils the hidden valley.
The mediaeval farmhouse on the hill,
The new estate that nestles in the fold,
Alike glow luminous and ghostly

My dog on his nightly exploratory prowl
Sniffs the damp hedgerow, the fascinating scents,
Gives a wide nervous berth to the badger's gap,
Sends some small scared creature scurrying.

In the distance a dog-fox barks,
And a sad cow mourns her young.
We head for home and bed.

[6]

Advent

Dark arboreal filigree against a pearly mackerel sky.
The winter beech glows copper in the thin light.
Festoons of smoky clematis snow-light the copse and
　　hedgerow,
And the thorns drip in abundance their bounteous berried
　　blood.

"What damn-fool notions brought our forebears this far
　　north",
Groans our youngest with the wisdom of eight years,
Shivering as he hatches his latest game and scheme,
And recalling our sole summer in Provence.

We smile and count the shopping days to Christmas,
And await the solstice,
And the coming of the sun,
And of the Son.

[8]

Pollen-fever

My garden is a flowery mead,
My head is filled with pollen-loaded drowsiness.
Work beckons but the call is faint.
I want to sit in the sun and dream.

[9]

Learning

Kick the dog day

The sky rides high for a late October day.
Small summer-white clouds in a bright blue heaven.
The distant trees glow softly like a once beautiful, now fading
 redhead.
The air is dank with rotting leaves, strange fungi, and bonfires
 still to come.

That black rascal,
Last remaining child of my middle age,
Naive, shrewd, cunning, foolish, wise,
That amiable nuisance, my dog,
Lurches ahead with excitement.
For a brief hour, he can forget that he is the fool of the family,
And become once more
The primitive hunter, pack scout, terror of the wild.

We plunge beneath the cathedral gloom of trees.
Today I do not wish to socialise,
Exchange mild banter with my fellow guardians of the canine
    race.
Today, if the dogs fight I shall kick their bottoms and utter
    foul oaths,
The well-constructed bourgeois face will slip,
Bewildering those I meet.

Today I hurt.
My body aches with loss,
New loss, old loss, primeval loss.

The wind grows chill.
The distant spring does not belong to me.

[10]

Transference

I would like to walk with you in the long grass,
To tread the hay underfoot,
And smell the warm lush scents of summer.

I would like to talk with you of things that catch my fancy,
Not seriously, solemnly, spread out for dissection,
But lightly with laughter and teasing,
And that gentle flirtation that needs no consummation.

But instead I sit here alone in the sun,
And you in your room attending
To the next sad tiresome soul.
And I must go on pretending
That you are just a dull grey man in a dull grey suit
No more than any other.

[11]

Return

The colours of the moss agates in the jeweller's window are beautiful,
As are the green and gold autumnal hues of the lakeside trees.
In this rock-strewn place of hills and streams, I found my first freedom,
Experienced the first full adult surge of sexuality.
In this Celtic fringe land, my Celtic blood first stirred.
There was magic here.

I did not know then that the magic was also within,
Enough to fight a way through the pain.
Enough to build a new life, and new lives,
To grow flesh on the bone-deep wounds.

But what now? The surge tide is ebbing.
The pain was no figment, the memory did not lie,
Enhancing perhaps, distorting a little here,
But there protecting, casting a dimming veil.
It was no dream, dispersing in the clear full light of day.

Shall I yet be overcome at the end?
Or can I find another magic place that will aid me in the dying?

[12]

Courtship Dance

Come into my parlour says the spider to the fly.
Come up and see my etchings sometime.
She leans against the cushions and smiles through half-closed
 eyes
And swings her elegant foot with its needle-sharp toe and
 dagger-sharp heel

And he, the gentle fresh young man,
Not long severed from his mother's apron strings,
Stares wide-eyed and open- mouthed
That so exotic a creature should deign to notice him.

Stop! Hold back, I want to shout,
You are too soft and young.
There are other games to play, other prizes to be won.
But already 'tis too late; the scene is set.
The courtship dance already has begun.

And what come next as the silken threads grow tighter?
Six months of married bliss, and a lifetime of hell.
While she grows sleek and petulant, and he an empty husk.

[13]

Adolescent Lacuna

This alien lunar landscape was our kingdom,
With twisted, strange moon-dusted flowers starred.
We wandered in this hilly in-between place,
Safe from our elders' pressures, lies and lunacies,
Sharing our fantasies of what might be,
Exploring our sexual, chaste, ambiguous intimacy,
Feeling, breathing, being, living a respite,
In this soterial haven ere battle was joined.

[14]

May Song

May's a merry month.
I can feel the garden growing
With the moisture, warmth and sun.
The choir of chestnut candles shouts with joy.
The hedgerow is awash with umbelliferous bridal froth.
The countryside's a tapestry of vibrant, singing green.

May's a cruel month.
It's the month when my son died.
Though twenty years and more have passed, the grieving has
    not ceased.
The purple lilac still it makes me weep.
And inwardly the heart it still is aching,
In May, the merry month of May.

[15]

A Small Death and Resurrection

Today I am mad,
And with consuming, gut-grinding anger,
And with the cold rage of deep affront.
Because their way is the only way,
They alone have the answers,
And are sole possessors of the truth.
And they cannot listen, and they will not hear,
And are deaf to understanding.
And they bruise the antennae, break the fingers, crush the toes
Of those who travel other paths, and different ways
Along the Way.

I am haunted by three corpses littering the road,
A badger, a fox and a God-knows-what,
Victims of the pressed-steel monsters which thunder down the highway.
Each day they become more filthy, bespattered, anonymous.
In my fantasy, I go out at dead of night
With my spade to bury them decently.
In reality I too am alway hurrying -
To keep an appointment, to meet a deadline, get home to bed.
So I grieve and pass by.

24

This morning, in the thin, sound-muffling mist,
I disturbed a solitary crow,
Breakfasting on the remains of the God-knows-what.
Then in the sunlit valley, I watched a flock of rooks
Soaring in the thermals, high above the shining river,
Lazy joy in their outstretched wings.
Sighing, I let go my rage and grief,
And allowed the gentle healing to pour in.

[16]

Thankfulness

Pink copper leaves against a bright blue sky.
If this be my last spring, I shall drink it in with gratitude.
Drink in the sun on my face, the honey-scented air,
Drink in the hedgerow flowers, violet, campion, celandine,
And the intricacy of the blatant dandelion.

Drink in the flower-faced children,
And the weary parental love that underpins their lives.
Feel gratitude for the love which brought forth children and
    their children,
For the warmth of home, and dogs, and work well done;
The shared bed, shared sadnesses, shared pain.
To say, as George Fox said, with contentment at last,
'I was glad that I was here.'

[17]

Boiling-point

All my life I have weighed my words, fearful of giving
 offence,
Given others space, supported and nurtured,
Played the stooge, leaving them the limelight.
To what end?
In the faith of mutuality,
In the hope that some day, someone would do the same for
 me.

And did they? Did they hell!
They sucked me dry, and then cried out for more.
Complained when the stream ran dry.
Left me exhausted, spent, to find what nourishment I could,
Until the next onslaught.

I was never to be the bride, the pretty one,
Find a lover, have children of my own,
Have space for those small, precious acts of creation.
My coat was of grey stuff,
Worthy, serviceable, to last forever.
No colour, no fancy frippery for this good girl.
That was not the game plan.

Well ... not any more!
You go it wrong, and so did I.
With time the power balance shifts.
God give me restraint - and forgive me my sins.

[18]

Episode

The car rushes through the night.
Our sensitive, perceptive little mouse
Drives with precise, top-executive verve.
The street lights reflect, flying-saucer, shooting star, in the
 black sky.

Is Sister Jane aware?
But that wise old, whisky-imbibing Irish doctor nun
Is long past shocking. And she loves us.

I curl up close, head into your shoulder,
My brother, father, mother, child.
No, not husband, not this time round.

The boundaries dissolve.
I lose myself in your darkness.
Lord, have mercy on us. Christ have mercy on us.
Lord have mercy on us. I am back home.

The city of dreaming spires looms near. The commercial
    signs glare.
The fast-greying frau sits up with a sigh,
Straightens her skirt, straightens her face,
Submerges her tears into their well.
We are back in the here-and-now.
The evening's gaiety is at an end.

It has been good seeing you again.
Shalom, till next time, next year.
My love to my witch-sisters under-the-skin.
Shalom. Shalom, my dear,
Blessed be.

[19]

Lesson Learned

In my youth, real men had tattoos along their forearms,
Fags hanging from their lips,
And swore mindlessly, interminably,
Every other word a b ... or f .....

The girls in their brazen youth,
Bleached their hair, and waggled their hips,
And raucously brayed their burgeoning sexuality,
Fuelling the gaggle of whores in Shepherds' Market.

Ten years on, hair lank,
In grubby pinny and down-at-heel shoes,
They endlessly moaned their lot,
Upbraided and cuffed their young,
Who early learned to duck.

Is it any surprise then that,
When talk turned to marriage and such,
I lifted my head, looked about me
And thought, 'No way!'.

[20]

Loss

Grandfather

The fields are scattered golden with radiant, upturned
    dandelion faces.
The pears in the hedgerow are heavy laden with white snow
    clumps of blossom.
No more will the old man totter down the garden path in his
    early morning carpet slippers,
To peer at the church clock tower through the orchard trees,
Sniff the moist country scents,
And bemoan the state of his cabbage patch.

No more will the young men writhe and squirm under his
    whiplash tongue,
Drawn unwillingly, inexorably into argument,
Knowing that, right or wrong, they will inevitably lose.
No more will his daughters silently fume
As he bullies, cajoles, manipulates his wife into providing his
    needs,
While grumbling, protesting, giving as good back,
She does his bidding,
Knowing as they do not,
The frightened small boy beneath the grizzled skin.

He gave us much.
To one a profession,
Another a life-long obsession,
A third a helping hand at time of need,
A fourth the necessary spur to achieve.

And now we shall dance to his tune no more.
The centre of the web is empty, the spider gone.
In vain we await the silken steely twitch,
And feel bereft.

[21]

Empty Chairs

The golden glowing globe sinks down to meet the dark mass
 of the hill.
The chill mist rises, dispels the lingering warmth of day.
My fat round apples swell visibly,
And the plum-drunk wasps can manage but the drowsiest
 warning buzz.
Only the bees dart purposefully among the self-sown purple
 loosestrife.

Last year those gaudy garden chairs were occupied by the
 old couple,
Resting their weary limbs after the day sight-seeing,
Endlessly commenting to each other in their customary
 fashion,
On all that had, and was, and would be,
Happening to them and theirs.

How odd that scene can never be repeated.
How odd that I should so much miss
The old man's interminable talk.

[22]

Epitaph for Lal

This is not him, this old, cold, grey shell.
He was so quick, so full of life and busyness.
The slick back chat, the next job to be done,
Going through the house 'like a dose of salts'
In the words of that woman, his lady,
Turning aside with a wry smile, a deft practised phrase,
Those barbed verbal shafts which were her way of loving.

But he loved her, protected and cherished her,
Avoided deep wounds by his very speed.
And created space and freedom for himself.

Perhaps that is why a faint, sardonic smile
Still lingers on his face.
Escape at last!

[23]

Manic Mourning

Sun and rain, cold, warmth and showers.
Heigh-ho the Spring is sprung.
But that man-Jack, Jack-in-the-box,
Where is he?
He will spring no more;
Nor slowly gently push aside the sodden earth to rise once
    more,
Like my green-speared daffodils.
His worn-out cast-off carapace
Is crumbling where it lies.
Ashes to ashes, dust to dust and back to the nitrogen cycle.

So,
Let's go out on the town.
Let's all have a ball.
Let's spend a little or spend a lot,
For life is for living
And money for burning.
They're no use once you're dead.

[24]

Gwladys

She totters down my garden steps
Like a jaunty young cock bird in bright plumage,
In her shoulder-bare, purple top and snake-print pants,
Barbaric gold belt and mules,
With coyly clumsy flirtatious aside
To elicit the caring sexual male response,
She totters down my garden steps
Behind that nimble young man,
My grown-up son, her grandson.
And I smile farewell,
At last, thank God, I can smile!

Thirty years ago, I was embarrassed.
Fifteen, found her pathetic.
Now, I can only marvel at the age-denying tenacity,
The sheer vitality,
Of the woman who can say,
With her lover of forty years not six months in his grave,
'I never wished that I was dead.
Sometimes that I had gone first.
But I know that when this dreadful time is gone,
There is still life ahead for me to live.
There are things still waiting for me.'

Only when I take his place
And hold her arm to cross the road
Do I feel the thin frailty.

[25]

Max

I had seen it coming, though in the event it came sooner than
    later.
I had prepared them all; prepared the children (children!)
Prepared that small minx, my granddaughter, whose playful
    friend he was.
(She took it with the grave naivety of the very young -
He won't bark so loud when he is dead, will he?)
I had prepared us well,
So why did it still hurt like hell.

It's not as if he were a very satisfactory dog,
Not like his predecessor.
Now he was a giant - intellectual, aristocratic, a prince
    among dogs.
This one was always a scruffy mutt, a guttersnipe, a wild
    welsh boyo of a dog,
Born to roam his native hills, chivvying the cattle, herding the
    sheep,
Defending his homestead with all too much gusto.

Children's playmate, family butt, companion of the
    countryside,
Half child, half lover and, at the end, my faithful shadow.
His warmth, unstinted, undeserved, it grounded us.
I miss him!
And now my home is full of dog-shaped holes.

Our Daughter Died

Elegy

God plucked a flower ere it faded,
Leaving us bleeding and bereft.

I shall always think of you, my brown-haired feral daughter,
Striding along the beach, long hair streaming in the wind
With your dogs, old Tom and little Georgie Girl,
And the ghosts of Bella, Max, and Leo your true lover,
And gentle giant Grendel,
Your canine brother.

As the wild silver salmon fights its way upstream,
Leaping the obstacles
To return to its spawning ground,
Then, task accomplished, gently fades away,
So you too, having reared your young to adult independence,
Averted your face, and went on your way.

[26]

Melanie's Death

I thrash about, seeking solace
But there is none - only the void.
For the thin red cord of generation is snapped.
My daughter is dead.

No more sly, shared laughter at our family's mild madness.
No more sharing of dietary hints, and culinary know-how.
No more exchange of seedlings, and cuttings in their season.
No more bog-offs and the satisfaction of bounty-for-free.
No more bouncy dogs and their muddy paws, bringing chaos
    into my too-tidy home.

Her daughter and I clutch the frayed rope ends,
And each other's hands, with love,
Tears falling as we dance with her ghost

[27]

Regret

A year ago, at your grandmother's funeral,
I saw death in your face,
And thought it just the shadow of your mourning clothes.

While we struggled to complete the inventory of our things,
Bought for your inheritance,
A voice kept nagging
"Hurry, hurry, It's later than you think."

I never thought of you.

[28]

Clearing-Out

Bags here, bags there,
Clothes, books, towels, sheeting.
All recycled, nothing wasted.
Off to the charity shops.

You would have approved of that.
But God, how much it hurts,
As we slowly dismantle your life,
As we discard the last remnants of you.

[29]

Bereavement Aftermath

I want to be gone. I want to be shot of it all.
I want to be free of this accumulation of THINGS
Furniture, pictures, clothes,
Books—ah, perhaps not books.
Some of value, some rescued from charity shops, all with
    meaning.
The detritus of a long life,
Gathered over the years with recognition, discrimination and
    love.

They remind me too much–of past times, of people now gone.
Of joys, yes, but too much of sorrow and pain;
Of hopes and aspirations now trickled into dust.
I am tired of carrying memories. Oh, for the dyslexic's gift!

The young have their own lives,
Their world is not mine.
They do not need to be lumbered
With burdens not of their choosing,
With expectations, perspectives that belong to another time,
Do not need to waste half their energy, half their life,
Resisting, expelling, the poison of a dubious inheritance,
As we did.

Once I dreamed of a sea-side, sand scoured beach hut,
Now a clean, anonymous modern flat will do.
It was Caitlin, Dylan's widow, who wrote of leftover life to kill.
A tiresome, destructive woman said Vernon, their friend, our
    neighbour,
And I believed him,
But I understood just how she felt

[30]

Secrets

Where were you when I looked to find you?
Searched every nook and cranny of your haunts?
No whisper of your presence did I find there
To moderate the pain that you had gone.

Why did you come to find us in that strange land
Of warmth and sunshine, darkness and of pride?
A land that you had never known in real life.
A land where your face fitted like a native,
Out of the blue you came to us one day.

Suddenly I knew what you never told us.
The jigsaw pieces all fell into place.
I wish you could have shared it while you lived here,
But know it was not your secret to betray.

You were always private, protective of what mattered.
You did drop hints but would not follow through.
I was stupid not to let my thoughts go further.
It never occurred to me to even wonder.
Would I have guessed if you had not been just my daughter?
Would I have loved you less if I had known?

I can smile now at what seems so clear and obvious,
Regret I cannot talk it through with you.
I would have liked to make it all much simpler,
But am glad that I finally knew.

Love is not something to be regretted,
Whatever curious paths it opens up.
Without it we remain unformed, unfinished.
With it we leave indeed a legacy,
And the legacy you have left us is good.

[31]

Gwalia

Seascape

Satin-blue sea, still as a millpond.
Gentle waves curl and splash on to the sand.
A flock of gulls doze on the incoming tide,
Unobserved by the skittering illegal dog pack who,
For a brief half-hour, dance with excitement and enjoy their
    canine selves.

The tawny tower glows in the setting sun.
A solitary yellow rose lingers in the hedge.
I wish my daughter were here!

[32]

The Strand, Swansea

On the bombed sites, the willow herb grows.
The once-thriving Strand is abandoned and decayed,
Crumbling; windows cracked and eyeless.

Up the narrow steep lane, the buddleia thrives,
Its purple pendants glowing.
Its roots seek their nourishment in the walls, nooks and
    crannies,
Searching, binding, knotted.

The butterflies gather in droves,
And the hurrying pedestrian sneezes.

[33]

St. Non's Bay

The wind always blows,
And the sea crashes and soughs on the rocks below.
But here there is a deep and curious peace,
As if St. Non and St. David laid their hands on this shore
And created an eternal heavenly moment,
Time without end.
Amen.

[34]

Spring Holiday In Pembrokeshire

Between the land and sea and sky
There is a wide, wide space.
Between the sea's thunder and the crying of the gulls
There is a deep, deep silence.

The wind bites the face and ears,
Blows round and under and through,
Emptying the mind, cleansing the soul,
The wind of God.

The land smiles in the warm spring sunshine,
And the gorse smells of coconut.

[35]

Hiraeth

Out there the surf pounds against the sea-wall.
Out there the ships dip from crest to trough in the storm,
The wind howls and the lighthouse earns its keep.

Out there my friends get on with their lives in my absence.
Some are gone, dead or departed.
Some, I know, knew I loved them;
Some I never told, but they were part of the tapestry of my
    world.
Now that tapestry grows thin and tattered.

I never meant to stay in this lush and cossetted hypocritical   land.
I need to be out there where the living is simpler, the people
    more vibrant, the joys more intense.
I need to be where the ocean beckons and the blood calls.
[36]

Cefn Bryn

I sit by the tomb of the great king and survey his lands.
White clouds in a clear blue sky throw shifting shadows
    across the estuary,
Across the salt-marsh where the sheep graze,
Across the neat small fields with their scattered white-washed
    farmsteads.

As I climb the grassy path, the ever-present wind
Blows through my hair,
Blows through the summer, sun-bleached moorland grass,
Blows with the scents and sea-spray of a thousand miles.

I walk as a wraith, wind-filled, among my forbears' ghosts.
As I tread the ancient ceremonial aisle
Time slips away, and then is now and here.
This landscape has entered my soul.

[37]

Bank Holiday

Milk-white sea and a milk-white sky.
Small ships glide like ghosts in the pale miasma.
Only the bodies on the shore-line are solid and real,
Shapeless and shapely, pink-brown to bronze, the old and
    the young,
So their chatter adds descant to the sea's rhythmic roar,
As the waves sparkle in the sun.

The elderly paddle, the young people preen.
Boys splash and whoop, small girls giggle and squeal,
Each flirting with the ripples,
Not yet with each other.

The dogs, heads seal-sleek, undulate and bound
Like fore-shortened Nessies,
As with their ancient, timeless time-without-mind ritual
The tribe foregathers to greet the incoming tide.

[38]

A timeless moment

The wind-ruffled waves splash and roar.
The wide expanse of beach is deserted.
Our small dog dances with joy,
Finding treasure trove in seaweed, stick and plastic bottle,
Scattering the paddling gulls who flap lazily, unconcernedly,
    out of reach.

The damp sand is punctured by a myriad of tiny holes,
The burrows of worms the fishermen dig for bait.
Our feet crunch on shells - last homes of creatures whose
    progeny still thrive and multiply out there,
Leaving their remains to be ground into yet more, ever finer,
    sand.

Time stretches endlessly back and fore.
We are but a small moment in the ongoing saga.

The town across the bay is obscured. It looks like a patch of
    rain.
Home for tea.

[39]

Contentment

A sun-kissed, God-given, blessing of a day,
An absence of breeze, air sparkling like wine.
A faint haze blurs sea into sky.
Everywhere, pools of daffodils, scatterings of celandines,
Gorse buds bursting forth.

We amble down an old familiar track - (I hardly need my
 stick!),
Sit to view the cliffs, the slade, the distant fishing smacks,
Eat a leisurely lunch of local cheeses and ham
At the much improved, extended cliff-top caff.
Watch the birds as they perch in defiant pairs
Along the ridged roofs and telephone wires.
Smile at the dogs, paused for coffee with mistress,
Exuberance vying with patient waiting.

The oh-so-new, oh-so-blue little car purrs along like a dream,
And the rare, rose-red magnolia blooms in full glory.

[40]

The Wheel Turns

Aubade

The landscape smiles in the opalescent Spring sunshine.
Snowy sloe blossom lights up the still bare hedgerow twigs.
A soft green haze blurs the wands of willow,
And the gorse is bursting into flower.

Only in my dreams am I still young and fecund,
Suffused by a gentle glow
As I recall the soft warm bodies
Of toddlers, puppies and Prudence, the cat.
Basking in the naive contentment of our bare-board life,
Before it all was shattered,
Before ...

The wheel of existence turns;
Winter glides into spring,
The earth's death and resurrection,
A part of our life too,
Inexorably the same, inexorably different.
Nothing static, no turning back.

Now is the turn of our young ones,
Another, other world.
I watch - and pray.
I shall not see the end.

[41]

A parent's tale

Why have babies?
Why this deep, relentless aching in the gut
Which nothing will assuage?

Children are just trouble.
As infants they deprive us of our sleep,
Intrude uncannily on our sexual lives,
They shred our nerves and patience to a frazzle.
They deprive us of our leisure, absorb our income,
Organise our lives around their needs.

The boredom of endless evening PTAs!
The enforced confrontation with tired lethargic teachers,
The anxiety as we wait for the late-night click on the latch,
Our concern at the company they keep.

But ... they are our future.
They are the part of us which goes on into the unknown.
They mediate our fear of annihilation,
Of leaving not a trace of our existence here.
With them, there is something will remain.

And not just us, but those who went before us.
Genetics is a curious endeavour,
As we recognise in this small and unformed soul
Its grandparental features, another's restless drive,
A shape of brow, a curious sense of humour,
A talent only latent in its time.
What will emerge from this unique new package?
Worth carrying on if only to wait and see.

They amuse us, delight us, enrich us, enrage us,
They give our lives a meaning beyond ourselves.

Then, however mixed our feelings,
We have to let them go again,
To become the person each alone embodies,
Trusting that we have prepared them for their separateness,
To find their place, their loves and their own struggles,
Just as we did.

[42]

Cousins

The young woman walks proudly down the aisle,
Bonneted head held high,
Resplendent in her crimson gown.
She sees us, beams, pauses for a camera shot, moves on.
A moment of triumph, hard-won and well-deserved,
A success achieved against the odds.

Her cousin, ten years younger,
Writes, texts, daily, her friend in Afghanistan,
Out of compassion, knowing the score.
An idealist, she hopes to join the band of brothers.
My guts are in pain.

[43]

Graduation Day

A summer's day. A great day. Graduation Day.
The rite of passage, high point of triumph,
For a whole cohort of our young.
We bask in the glow of their celebration.

We sit briefly by the river, admire the view.
A gaggle of young mallards paddle by,
Not quite adult, still with their sibling group,
Proud parents watchful at their side.
We smile - 'A good breeding season, this summer.
No, sorry, we have no bread for you today!'

A convoy of young men, some barely out of school,
Ride out in their armoured car
And are blown to smithereens.
'Sorry, we have no cash to buy you the gear you need.
Hard luck, lads! Do your best with what you've got!'

[44]

Josh at eighteen

A young lad.
Quiet, pleasant, no great intellectual.
He did not shine at school.
One of the crowd, glad to be unnoticed,
Happy to get by without trouble.

He found a group which gave him status,
A group of friends in which all felt valued.
They bothered to give him training,
Bothered to notice,
Made him feel he had something to offer.

What else could he do,
Where else could he go?
A lamb to the slaughter,
Thrown into the lion's den of the Afghan hills.
Inadequately equipped, under-resourced,
Supported by the powerful camaraderie,
He faced his fear as he had been trained to do.

What now, limbless, traumatised,
Fighting for very life.
Was it worth the sacrifice?
Like Hell!
Not my son - but they are all my sons,
And they deserve something better.

[45]

Easter

The fires of youth have left but a few glowing coals.
The world out there Is not my world.
'It is not the world I had hoped for,
Not the world I worked for,'
Says my social worker friend.
And I, too, do not much care for it.

The natural world, now that is a different matter.
The long grey winter has slipped away,
And all is green and vibrant,
Shimmering with new life.
The trees in bloom,
The birds busy, eating all on offer,
My newly planted border
Effulging with vitality.

I listen to my neighbours' sad distressing tale.
A sick young man, struggling to keep sane,
Made ill by the chaotic tensions of family life,
Unrecognised, unspoken, but still felt.
The scapegoat to be fought and kicked.

Easter - we celebrate the Resurrection.
A statement, says my favourite theologian, that
"God can make Heaven out of a Hell of a mess."
I offer signs of hope,
And pray.

[46]

Lunch at Oxwich Bay

As we swoop down the precipitous winding hill
I recall the exhilaration of our first ever ride there.
Would our ancient basic car ever manage the return!
The excitement of the path across the marsh
Between banks of tall plumed grass,
Against a backdrop of virgin-forested hill.
An exotic, foreign place.

I sit and view the bay between the palm trees,
Watch the tiny figures at the far edge of the low tide,
And the small dogs racing madly around with joy.

The wedding party passes our window.
White fur capes and fascinators to mark the occasion,
Male buttonholes of daffodils for Dewi Sant.
A tribal celebration.
A young girl cavorts in her traditional national dress,
Reminding me of another more sober child
In steeple hat, red skirt and red plaid shawl -
Lifetimes ago.

The waiter enquires - shall you be joining us for dinner?
I explain the long residence in these parts, the second home,
    the visits.
It is good to come back, he says - and means it.

At the crossroads our friends' old house still stands,
Built with love by his own hands,
But now divided into two, half up for auction,
Changed beyond recognition.
All gone - friends, girl, sense of home.

Two years ago, the marsh was drying out,
To the locals' dismay.
Now, after a season of interminable rain, of widespread
    floods,
There is standing water there again.
The wildlife will love it, the naturalists rejoice.

Today's car clings to the contours with sure-foot ease.

[47]

Time moves on

Amid the grimy red-brick terraces
There were other forms of life:
The brewers' mighty Shires
With their swaying sensuous rumps,
The milkman's placid workhorse,
The rag-and-bone man's scrawny nag.

Great flocks of sparrows
Swirled in crowds above the chimneys,
Straddled along the telegraph wires,
Settling to peck crumbs amongst the cobbles,
Cheerful and self-contained.

Today in my village garden
We have a now rare pair of sparrows.
She bathes in the little fountain,
Spreading and fluttering her feathers,
While he stands proudly alert.

A fledgling bumbles around -
From wall to shrub, from ground to tree-top,
Exploring this fascinating, beckoning new world,
Blundering barn-ward, retreating to cover,
Basking in the sun.

I think of our youngest,
Recently quit the nest,
Working hard, playing hard,
Saying 'yes' to life,
With bright wide-open eyes,
A handsome plumage,
And a shrewd protective innocence.

We chase away our neighbour's cat.

[48]

Blue Devilled
[49]

Grief

They say grief does not kill.
'No one dies of a broken heart.'
They do not understand.

True - death does not come swift and cleanly
As one might wish.
But slowly, insidiously,
As one fights back the tears, suppresses the sobs,
Fails to breathe deeply
For fear of the howls that might escape.

One's chest becomes stiff,
And one's heart misses its gentle massage,
One's body is held rigid for fear of collapse,
And the heart works harder to pump its vital fluid.

Your blood pressure is up, they say,
Have some pills to make it better.
You have coped so well, they say,
Meaning, we prefer to think that way,
Too frightened to look beyond the social face,
Too close to home for comfort.
Don't really want to know.

God damn them all!

[50]

Christmas blues

Beyond the devastating lethal-yearning misery,
Between the bouts of racking meaningless sobs,
A gleam of insight dawned.

As now, when it is the loving kindness which evokes the storm,
Is that how it was then?
Was it the love, the kindness, the wished-for undeserved presents
Which eroded my defences,
Released the pent-up misery,
Hoping it could be understood,
Contained, soothed and transformed
So that real feeling life could begin again.

But no, this was a time to be jolly. Jig, jig, jiggety-jig,
Don't be a silly girl, nothing to cry about.
See what Santa Claus has brought you.
All these lovely things. Aren't you lucky?
And tomorrow - back to old clothes and porridge,
And the tensions, lies, pretences,
Ill-understood but, confusingly, still felt.

Was this why I have always hated Christmas?
Where's the reality of celebration?
Is this why the infant on our card,
New-minted, trusting and serene,
Is this why he makes me cry?

[51]

Having it all

Last evening we changed our routine
And visited some old friends.
He now frail and palsied, with breaking bones,
But as ever warm, courteous and dogged
With a stoical courage and smile.
She a little confused,
Surprised at the departure of energy,
Missing the buzz of committees, bridge parties and travel.

We exchange news of family and friends,
Far-flung and out of reach,
Even the grandchildren have their own lives,
Sea and sand no longer the lure.

Usually a source of pride,
She voices her concern for two young boys,
Both parents high achievers in their different professions,
Father rarely at home, Mother in demand.
They have good schools, caring god-parents,
But one is small and thin and struggles ...

When young, she had the offer of heart surgery.
Refused it since there were young children, a recently
    widowed mother,
Her own needs a tiresome blip in the full domestic round.
She survived to become the matriarch of her clan.
I listen and hear the unvoiced connection.

I think of those other two children,
Father a secular missionary to Africa,
Changing the world while the native plutocrats swell their
    Swiss bank accounts.
The stress of living with danger,
The disruption of education,
The breakdown of marriage.
Their grandmother also grieves.

Today I am tired and weary.
Four children left with the task of constructing their lives
From the crumbs falling off the table.
How do you love fully when at your heart is an ever-leaking
    sieve?
Isn't life difficult enough without such burdens from the start?

When we honour those who achieve
Publicly - for the common good,
We need to ask,
And who pays the price?

[52]

Denial

Don't think about it, dear, said the woman,
Here's a nice bit of fish for your supper.
A good meal solves it all.
And it worked for her. Until the end
She was cheerful, ebullient, and warm.

Don't think about it, said her son.
That was yesterday. It is over -
Sunk costs - why dwell on it.
Ahead are new thoughts to think, new things to make,
A brave new world to create,
That will solve all our ills.

Don't think about it, dear,
Said her granddaughter.
I escaped from the muddle and the mess,
To make a new life, find a new partner, make a new home.
You too need to do the same.
Put it behind you and forget.

But what of those who could not do this;
Who were left to feel the pain,
Disentangle the muddle, shoulder the depression,
And no one to share it with.

If you cannot mourn, you do not learn.
And not everyone can forget.

What of the child, left hurt and bewildered,
Denied the help needed to process it all,
Struggling to create a new, different life,
But stuck, stuck, stuck.
As the opportunities slid by,
A casualty, a failure, a scapegoat.

[53]

Old Age

The holiday was great.
Coming home was not.
I do not want to live here any more!
I cry out in despair
But my husband will not hear.
He loves this house and garden I have made -
And so did I.

But it is too full of ghosts,
Of gatherings and people,
Of Sunday lunches, children and dogs.
Of past hopes and expectations,
Of friends and neighbours,
The currency of life as it is lived.

Each artefact was gathered,
From antique fair and shop,
A discovery, a delight,
Source of interest and pleasure,
Risking taste and judgment,
Fuelling one's knowledge,
Adding layers of meaning to mundane domestic life.

Even the plants have their history.
A recalcitrant Saintpaulia, a cast-off from my mother,
Bloomed with enthusiasm here.
Now I have sixteen, cousins of that first,
All different and demanding of my care.

The garden it just happened,
It grew bit by bit
From a wilderness of bugle and riotous buttercup.
Now the trees create coolness,
There's a focus for each season.
An oasis of lush greenness
Gives forth foxglove, clematis, rose.
There's no room for anything new.

Now I am just weary,
Needing to shed it.
The absences pain me.
I have done what was needed.
I need to let it go.

I need to forget the years,
I need a blank canvas,
I need a new body,
I need a new life.
Perhaps I just need to go.

[54]

Cry from the heart

I had looked forward to some feeling of contentment,
A cradling in the soft glow of the ending,
A sense of life well-lived, job well-enough done,
A legacy scattered with appreciation.

I had not reckoned with the searing sense of loss
Of a limb torn prematurely from the trunk.
I had not reckoned with the relentless surge of anger,
The void of feeling cheated, violated.

I had not reckoned on the draining of the light,
The ebbing of colour till all a dreary grey.
I miss the surge of love, of thankfulness,
I crave the voice, the sense of presence and of scent.

What was it all about then, all that struggle
To give life, to nurture, to provide,
To hold back one's own desires and strivings
For the sake of one's young and their vulnerable lives.

I thought my maternal love would be enough
To protect, to give a sound base from which to fly.
I failed in spite of all my efforts.
It is hard to make something positive of all that.

It is hard now to hold on to basic trust
Hard to believe in a beneficent God.
Hard to feel it was worth all that terrible effort,
Hard not to feel abandoned in our need.

Hard not to sink now into despair.
Not quite the end I had ever envisaged.
So much for one's hopes and expectations!
God knows, they had been little enough.

[55]

Ending

I should like to drift out on the ebb tide
With the soft sea shoosh in my ears,
Leaving my loved ones in a good place,
Knowing they have been loved.

Instead I am land-locked in this decrepit hulk,
Too tired to be useful,
Too well-maintained to disintegrate.
Stuck.

Coming into this world was protracted and painful,
Rhythmically squeezed against a blocked tunnel,
Head banged against a brick wall
Until excitement and hope drained away,
And grateful oblivion stole in.

Will leaving this world be an equally tedious affair
Pointless and prolonged with the best of intentions.
I sometimes think the Good Lord could manage things better,
If He cared.

[56]

A magic house

My house is a shape changer.
From hunting lodge to wayfarer's inn,
From village pub to rural slum,
From builder's wreck to bourgeois des. res.
The magic remained intact.

My house has elastic walls.
Spacious for two, though books burst the seams.
Seats eleven for a lunch, embraces dozens for drinks.
Comes alive when full of people and noise.
Sighs with relief when quiet is restored.

It has many ghosts.
Footsteps tread the boards, they walk the stairs.
No one at home next door.
Indifferent to us, no message, no threat.
Cider jars in their hands?
And what of the blue lady who haunts the garden?
Disappears round corners into a blank wall.
Mistress, maid, the Lady of the coven?
Ages ago, but when?

We are but newcomers, transients.
When the walls were stripped,
The house, it silently screamed.
Shed its blue-blood dust quietly, in despair.
We coughed and choked, sickened and vertiginous,
Weakened and despairing ... until ...

We finally got the message,
Knew how it felt.
Covered the walls as our ancestors wont,
Staunched the flow, filtered the air,
Allowed it to breathe again.

Now it smiles,
Welcomes our presence,
Wraps us in safety as of old.

They are not very bright, these humans,
But if you persist, they can learn.
Now we can relax for a few more aeons,
The magic still intact.

[57]

Growing up

Growing up

Rustling leaves against a bright blue heaven,
Cotton-wool clouds just out of reach.

Sand between toes, sand in the eyes,
Wind in the marram grass.
Great draughts of fresh air in sooted lungs,
Slimy seaweed, dangerous jellyfish,
A myriad different shells.
The wide, wide seashore and sky.

The damp ecstasy of a woodland grove,
Brook burbling under ferny fronds.
Autumn blackberries picked for free.
The dank and rotting scent of a lowland river.

The dusty magic of second-hand bookshops,
Listening with Dad to the wireless on Mother's night out -
Monday Night Theatre and the impact of new voices.
Concerts, broadcast and live,
And the visceral recognition of Beethoven, Debussy and
    beloved Chopin.

The scent of sun on moorland heath,
The shock of feet in ice-cold mountain pools,
The gift of a new landscape,
The solace of friends,
The infinite potential of other worlds
Out there!

[58]

Mother

You got a bad press from me - and you deserved it.
In your dotage you were a nightmare to be with.
You drove me to the brink, to the edge of breakdown.
I do not think you ever realised.
You soaked up all that was on offer
You stole his gifts, our time, our life.
There was no space for talking, even thinking
As we tried to fill your ever-leaking sieve.

But it was not always so, I remember,
You were good with babies, that I can recall.
Understood their needs, made them safe,
Brought the world to them coherently,
Played little games that made you both laugh.

Even later, you were a good home-maker.
Home was warm and cosy, curtained, a bright fire.
You were thrifty with what little you had,
And you had your creative side.

You collected objects that had some merit,
Made hats out of little bits of stuff,
Ran up clothes with fabric from the market,
Had enthusiasms for this and that.

What then went wrong between us?
You made a devastating error early on.
You went into denial and I hated that.
Could not forgive just being left alone
To howl myself to tearful desperation
And beyond - far, far beyond your reach.

I was not really the kind of child you wanted,
Dark curly hair, merry and bright.
I was my father's daughter, not just yours you know,
Sober, serious, pallid faced and sullen.
Not someone you could understand.

Separateness and difference were your undoing,
Not something that you ever recognised.
I dearly wish it could have been other.
It was tragic for both you and me.

[59]

Betrayal

Why did I care? Why did it hurt so much?
I don't know what's the matter with the child. Not eating her tea.
Just crumbling that nice piece of cake I baked.
Aren't I entitled to an evening out once a week!

Why did it hurt then - paralyse my guts? Fighting back the tears.
Truth to tell,
Once she had gone,
Peace reigned.

We sat in companionable silence, listened to the wireless.
A classical concert, World Theatre - a play.
We breathed out, the house relaxed.
As tension ebbed, calm drifted in.
It was possible to think -
And bedtime came too soon.

So why did it hurt?
Because I knew - though no one said it to me -
That it was a betrayal.
A betrayal of him, of me,
Of our family life together.
It was the start of the cracks opening up
Which got ever wider, would never be healed.
Of denial and obfuscation, of isolation,
Of retreat into fantasy.
It was the beginning of hell for us all.

[60]

Roots

'If you could choose where to live'
Asked my son - casually - at a large noisy lunch.
'Where would it be?'

No hesitation,
'Wales - at the coast.'
Thinking Gower or possibly Laugharne.
'We loved Carmarthen Bay when holidaying there.'
I smiled, thinking 'blood will out!'

'If not there, then where?'
'The border country'.
That curious mix of English and Welsh,
Some fine old buildings,
Quirky towns,
And few people.

My natural landscape,
Always on the border,
Never quite belonging.

But the lure of the sea is strong.
Perhaps a legacy of that Viking blood
Which gave me my father's white hair,
His stoicism,
And his quiet irony.

[61]

Relationships

Celebration

I thought I had forgotten how;
Lost the knack amid the aches and pains
And endless hypochondriacal concerns
Of the very old.

But his gentle, insistent hand
Stirred my memory,
Evoked the old familiar surge of ecstasy,
Blurring the boundaries in a flood of warmth
In a bodily, out-of-the-body dissolution
Into a passionate submission to the male Godhead,

I remembered M.
Whose husband died in her arms
At the peak of their encounter.
Shocking for her,
But what better way to be launched -
Catapulted - into eternity.

Slowly I drift back to earth.
I am still alive.
Now perhaps I can sleep.

[62]

Husband

You asked me how I rated you as a husband,
Your self-esteem ragged, and
Feeling your mortality.

I could have answered in truth - not easy!
Your dyslexic memory making you unpredictable, chaotic,
Forgetful of cherished plans and promises,
Focused on your personal inner world.

Then, to balance the scales,
I would have to add
Your energy, your spontaneity,
Your robust, idiotic optimism,
Your adventurous baking of bread,
Your creativity in matters of the mind.

Adventures in the outer world had been spoilt
By the bitter early separations.
Left you an anxious traveller,
Indifferent to the natural world, the landscape.
I found that hard.

But beyond all that
You met my needs at the deepest level,
Met my womanhood with your manhood,
Until - in the face of all my education -
I understood the nature of the human condition,
And could glory in it.

Your labour provided enough -
Of food and shelter and security -
So that together we could build a safe, if shaky, place
Each for the other,
And transmit those things of value to our young.

I think it is called love,
And a true marriage!

[63]

Son

Retiring in a year, you say
And I breathe a sigh of relief.
The working world has been hard for you.
At times I have feared for your survival,
My last remaining child.

You arrival was a gift from God,
A replacement for your dead brother.
A very different child,
Dark to his blondness,
Sensitive, and less robust.

I recall your newborn skinny limbs
And wobbly chin,
Your deep brown eyes
And wide smile as you learned to recognise
The radio's six pips.
A bright small boy!

You were an easy child
Cheerful and amenable.
Perhaps you knew I needed that.
I hope it didn't burden you.

A small version of your Dad,
You charmed the ladies in the Hall,
Charmed our local trader of sweets,
To sell them at cost price.
Charmed our grumpy gardener,
And the students mending their motorbikes
As you pottered in your red welly boots
To chatter and question.
You were a great chatterbox.

You were a handsome young man.
The photos remind me.
When the time came for girls to appear,
I knew I had to let you go
For you to find your own woman.
The inevitable pain of a parent.
But to cling is to destroy.

And now in middle age
A solid citizen, a safe pair of hands,
With integrity, judgment and insight.
Now as taciturn almost as my father,
Whose companionship your young self enjoyed.
Until alcohol, good company, lets loose once more,
The chatterbox of youth, the spinner of tales.

A Welshman in so many ways,
With deep feeling for the common good,
Despising the selfish infighting of barons,
The competitive scrabble to climb the ladder,
Refusing the tawdry lures of office.
A stimulator, reconciler.
Not an easy role.
I have watched and wondered,
Wished an easier milieu,
Glad of the wisdom and capacity to mature.

And now, what next?
I hope, more fun,
A flowering of those other bits
Pushed to one side by demanding roles.
I hope a long retirement
With room for real living,
And joy and gratitude.

[64]

Conference

The beautiful blonde American girl
Spews out her words with Gatling gun rapidity,
Obliterating space and difference and thought,
Obliterating the Other.
A stimulating, compelling lecture style
But in a small group - no way!

We each attempt to offer gentle comments,
Remarks towards other possible perspectives,
To no avail, unheard or then rejected.
The grey cloud of tedium descends.

I feel my anger slowly rising
And plunge in, ignoring courtesy to our guest.
I too have my personal agenda
And will not allow it to be silenced
Even if it contradicts the firm direction.

We are not a bunch of malleable students
But a group of old experienced survivors
Who had hoped to share their interests and queries.
I want to know what they too think.

Am I envious of her youth and beauty?
Youth, I think not. Mine was much too painful.
And beauty is always a delight,
Whatever package it arrives in.
Though it can be a dubious blessing
If relied on too much.

But that ability to hog the centre stage
That I do indeed admit to.
There have been so many such in my life.
When young I listened respectfully, with awe,
Seeking wisdom and some kind of confirmation,
Pinned down by courtesy and affection,
Willing to act the role of avid audience.

Alas, I am tired of the role of patient listener,
Of mirroring ideas and thoughts of others.
I am bored of always being the stooge.
I am weary of waiting for the silence,
The acknowledgment that I too might have a voice,
The opportunity to speak that never comes.

Now I recognise the scenario,
The empty void which never can be filled,
The need for an affirming mirror
Which wasn't there when desperately needed.
The sadness behind the facade.
Should I have been more patient?
At eighty, I no longer have time!

[65]

Mourning

Dear friend of my schooldays and turbulent youth,
I wish I could go with you down into the House of the Dead,
To hold your hand and meet again
Those others I have loved and miss so much.

But I am marooned here to go on living,
To cope with the glory of all those irritating and petty trivia -
The demands of the daily routine,
Of bathing and eating and laundry and cleaning
Which set the stage for our living
And create our precious small world.

I am so often tired and bored.
I have done it for eighty odd years.
I would like to lay it down.
But the Good Lord has other plans, I guess.
I wish they were clearer to me!

Another friend's son sends me a photo
Of his new small infant boy,
And thanks me for the gift of some clothes.
(I recall the joy and poverty of our own young parenthood,
And the generous part you played in it.)

I watch the royal tearaway at the end of his service furlough,
Looking stressed, exhausted and changed as he talks to the press.
I give thanks for the survival of our own young soldier,
That now I search through my catalogues for some clothes I can buy her,
Knowing I am perhaps the only one who would dare to take that risk!

W. thanks me for our lunch of his favourite lentil soup,
For a recent adjustment to his diet,
For rescuing his dangerously battered legs,
For remembering the details he continually forgets,
So he can go on writing - his endless endless writing.

Meanwhile I read - endless endless reading,
Of the far off distant past
Of origins lost in the mist of time,
And marvel at our ancestors - their courage and their daring,
Their creativeness, ingenuity, their capacity to survive,
As sophisticated in their way as we are now,
And the myriad incremental change which brought us to here.

We all contribute but a pennyworth.
In the making of the Kingdom of God.

[66]

Ann

I envied you, my cool, calm, elegant friend.
Envied you your social poise, your style,
Your sensible supportive mother.

I envied you your freedom to release yourself
From the engulfing ties of childcare
To pursue your own ambition.
To end a problematic marriage,
To find a mature partner.

You were generous to me,
Tolerant of my own alternative choices,
Sharing your home, not once but twice, at critical times.

Yet I never felt close for all my wanting it.
There must have been love, but was there liking?
I retreated, not wanting to intrude.

At last you made the journey - your only visit
To our distant country-mouse haven,
So alien to your svelte cosmopolitan niche.
By then, I felt I had had the better bargain,
An emotional, rich existence,
A sounder family,
The deep satisfactions of the profession you made possible,
A good life.

Now you are gone,
And with you so much of my history.
I grieve more than I had expected,
A hole rent in the weaving of my loom.
We were each of us women of our time.
I weep for what we had - and what we might have had.

[67]

For Mary

So you decided you had had enough,
That it was time to go,
And so you went.
A sensible, thought-out, well-planned decision
Worthy of the pragmatic, intelligent woman you were.

Oh dear, we all cried,
It shouldn't have happened in our community
We should have done something to prevent it.
Why didn't we see it coming?
Why didn't we make her feel we cared?

But I don't think that was how it was.
She had lived her life -
And a full and good one it had been.
But the young had fled to the far corners of the globe
Husband dead, just a daughter here and she not near.
Living in a world that was no longer hers,
Unsympathetic, alien - struggling with too much change.
And for what?

I envy you your courage.
Feel sad that I did not get to know you better.
I think we might have discovered much in common.
But the realities of old age are a burden
And the effort to do more than survive becomes too great.

I cannot go yet.
I still have a role to fill
And cannot abandon.
Shall I make the same decision,
Or just hope the Good Lord makes it for me
Out of compassion.

[68]

Insight

It is over.
The life we shared long gone,
Some major players now no longer with us,
And we the lingering last protagonists.

I used to envy you your lightness of touch,
Foil to my heavy burden of Celtic gloom,
Envied your flexibility, your love to roam
Across the globe,
In search of lotus land.

Now I understand so much,
The need to construct a safe post-natal world
In which we can be held, to grow and flourish.
The basic biology of our species.

Your mother was a feminist of her day,
A spunky woman, bright and no one's fool.
But she thought that babies were like kittens,
Content as long as watered, cleaned and fed
By whoever acting the temporary slave.
She did not know the need for firm containment,
Consistency and continuity of care,
From one who loves.

She condemned her child to be forever a wanderer,
Searching for something needed, unattainable,
Leaving her young to somehow muddle through,
With disastrous, painful consequences.

I stayed,
Trapped by my internal mother's angry depression,
Always secondary to her ongoing drama,
My own needs waiting to be met,
Waiting for the space that never came,
Waiting to learn who I was.

And the philosophers ramble on about Free Will.
What the hell do they know!

[69]

Kathryn

A frail, small child with wispy blonde hair.
A Welsh-Irish faery amongst the solid local clod-hoppers.

Trying to keep up,
Trying to fulfil the rivalrous expectations
Of the warring adults
Without the solid grounding that you needed.

Slowly you found your feet,
Found your own talent, found your drive.
Developed a carapace to see you through,
A stubborn prickly pride that was your shield
To protect the inner self against the blows.

You had a fierce devotion for your young
And fought your corner with vigour when it was needed.
You had a lousy hand of cards to play
But you played them with such courage and such pride,

And against the odds, against the good advice,
Something was created of great value,
A damaged life redeemed, a young life freed.
And you yourself grew in wisdom and in stature.

It was tough and it was tiring,
And it took its toll.
I wish you could have stayed a little longer
To appreciate the fruits of your endeavour.
I wish I could have given you more support
In that wearing final phase of your life here.

I wish it could have been easier, less a struggle,
But you did make something of it with your courage,
And I shall miss you.

[70]

Birthday Gathering at Nunney

Low winter sun on ruined castle walls.
Stark tracery of branches in a clear blue sky.
A rook flaps lazily and perches on the tree.

We huddle outside the village inn,
Awaiting the menfolk and their cars.
A pleasant event, a gathering of family,
An exchange of gossip, news and gifts,
Well chosen, well received.

Before, it seemed a hill too high to climb
But we made it, we played our part,
Glad to be included,
Enjoying friends and food,
Good to see the young so flourishing.

I sink on to the hard bench,
Too tired to zip my anorak,
Feeling a wreck - but no longer caring.

Soon be home. Another year?
Time alone will tell!

[71]

Women's Lot

'Don't ever grow old', said my mother-in-law
And I laughed, ruefully acknowledging her declining energy.
'I wish I had done more with my life!'
We rushed to reassure her, certain of our regard
As centre of the family web, husband's mainstay,
Successful entrepreneur in her small way.

I wish we had stopped, wished we had asked questions.
What was it she would have liked to have done?
I can guess now her frustrations as her time and strength
    slipped away,
The unused potential, the limitation of others' limitations,
The opportunities let slip so as not to disturb the peace.

We did not want to know, her granddaughter and I,
As we tidied up the kitchen after lunch,
Still playing the domestic role,
Resigned and contented enough with its rewards,
Still with time on our side.

Did she too feel the anger I now feel?
Does it always take a lifetime to learn one's strength?
Were the risks really too great?
Or did we under-estimate those we thought to serve?

'Parliament next?', I joke to my daughter-in-law,
Who feels guilt at all talk and no action.
A natural - feisty, pragmatic, feet-on-the-ground lass,
A woman of integrity.
Soon her daughters will be launched, the task all but over,
A time of freedom beckons ahead.
But wait - how long now before we oldies need her care?
And if not her, then who?

The family web enfolds us, and it traps us.
Without it we are isolates, half-formed.
It is the women who hold it all together,
Unrecognised, unpaid and undervalued,
A function quite unnoticed 'til not there.
The feminists do not begin to address it,
Make it worse by unrealistic expectations,
By denying our deep and basic biological selves.

In the light of ultimate things,
What, who, is it that matters most?

[72]

Universals

To the Hospital

The moon's a celestial balloon
Riding high in the November sky.
The landscape a monochrome etching
Stark bare branches on a milky wash.
The infinitely complex twiggy mesh of hedgerow
A squiggle source of delight.

The dawn comes up with copper streaks,
Illumines the puffball cloud with rosy flamingo pink
Against a deep clear blue ocean.
For minutes the shrub outside my window
Is an incandescent burning bush.

Why ever did we choose to travel
To that cold and lifeless place,
When the world here is so beautiful.

[73]

Christmas Story

We are all strangers in a foreign land
Searching understanding, the Ultimate Truth,
Visiting the Wizard of Oz,
Deciphering the Riddle of the Sphinx,
Seeking the Light of the World.

The Wise Men travelled before us,
Sustained by a portent and a hope.
Visited the King and his court,
But found there only envy, power and malice,
Experienced disquiet and moved on.

Finally what they found was just a baby,
An ordinary, unpanned, inconvenient baby,
Sleeping after its tiring passage into this world.
An exhausted teenage mother,
Quietly triumphant in her role,
Who had survived an experience testing her to her limits,
And brought forth a healthy child.

The shepherds were familiar with this scene.
It was a part of their lives, their skills,
To help their ewes produce their lambs each year,
They knew the cost, the mess and the joy,
The mystery, the miracle of birth.

And seeing, the Wise Men understood.
Knew the necessity of protection
Of that vast and vulnerable potential,
Knew what was needed was not the panoply of court,
But the quiet devotion of ordinary good parents,
Warned Joseph, and went on their way.

Joseph was no fool but a shrewd man
Not quite sure what he had got himself into,
But responding with a decent man's instinct,
Opted for the survival of wife and son,
And fled with them into Egypt.

[74]

Proclamation

I have been faithful to your Incarnation,
Responded as best I could
To the pulse of your creativity.

I have immersed myself in your landscape,
Revelled in your seasons,
The trees and plants, the flowers and fruits.
Been kind to dumb animals, especially the dogs,
(If less than kind to slugs and snails, alas!)
But saved many a wandering woodlouse and lost bee.
The birds in my garden are a source of delight,
As they forage for scraps and sunflower seeds.
(The food is good, but the service could be bettered!)

I have embraced the world of the flesh,
With its uncertainty, discomforts and its joys,
Revelled in those basic acts of passion
Which give meaning and structure to life,
Which herald the on-going creation,
The mingling of elements which re-makes the world anew.

I learned painfully to distrust and discount
The blasphemous abhorrence of the flesh
Preached by our elders,
Which would have destroyed our lives as it did theirs.
Made my peace with my rejected face.
Too like my father's!
What else did she expect!

Learned that being female is not about frills and bling
But about a certain receptivity,
A holding, containing, to then give out again;
The willingness to facilitate others,
Not always to hog the limelight.
To not feel threatened by the masculine imperative,
The necessary vital difference.

But we can only give
When we have been given,
And my judgments are too harsh.
Our needs must be met
Ere we can do that for others.

And now, what next?
My time is done.
Oblivion? A black hole?
A return to the formless stream of creativity which made our
    world?
Is there anything worth saving out of my small part?

As once I gave myself to the impersonal force of procreation,
Now I must needs sink into the great mystery.

[75]

Holding hands

Hold my hand for I am fearful,
Not of the prospect of death but of the process of dying,
Of the ebbing away of strength,
Of the capacity to say yea or nay,
Of the letting go of self-direction.
You too found that hard, I know.
Your stubborn independence was your treasure,
Hard won of necessity.
Lend me your hand, daughter mine,
Transmit to me the courage and stoicism
With which you met your end.

Let me take your hand, dear friend of my youth.
Though your dark hair is now as white as mine
And your fair skin brown and wrinkled as old leather,
As was your mother's, I remember,
But your hands and arms remain as delicate and slender as
    ever
Reminding me how much I loved you,
And how much I missed you when you went away.
Though our lives diverged, that bond remains,
A comfortable ease across the oceans and the years.

Grasp my hand, my love,
To steady my unsteady steps.
When we were young, it was you who sought my touch,
With all the new found pride of intimacy and possession,
While I held back, fearful for my separateness.
Now I am grateful for the unexpected understanding,
Which acknowledges the change and the need.

May I hold Your hand as I traverse this unknown journey?
In my teens I threw You out
Baby, bath water and all.
I wanted nothing of that judgmental, punitive God of my
    elders.
And quite right too!
But of course, slowly, insidiously You crept back,
In the landscape, flowers and trees,
In the sublime ocean of music,
In the casual kindness of Your angels,
In the myriad disguises of Your infinite creation,
In the splendour of Your Incarnation.

Now I understand that it is all quite beyond me,
My imagination too small for the reality,
I am free to feel like a child again,
Needing a parent's guiding hand,
No longer despising those inadequate formulations,
No longer fearful of the offered love,
Accepting my own frailty and need.
May I hold Your hand?

[76]

Mappa Mundi

A small and faded circle of vellum,
A map of the mediaeval world,
The place names not where we would put them,
The beasts and birds are weird, fantastical,
But the Christ rules over all,
The pilgrim destination of all mankind.

An insight into a long gone alien world.
A miracle of survival,
Made possible by the loving care of men unknown
Fortunate living far from the seats of political power and strife
In an unimportant rural back-of-beyond.

It did for them the task that we all have
To integrate our understanding of our world
Into some kind of coherent whole.
It relieves our existential anxiety,
It keeps us feeling safe in a threatening world.

But perhaps our maps, our modern Mappa Mundi
Are as quirky and inadequate as was theirs.

[77]

The search

Why do you seek me in these stone-cold, dark and dusty
    places.
When out there is sun and light and air,
Where the grass grows lush upon my skin,
And the water springs pure and clear from deep inside my
    body.
Where birds soar with lazy ease about their business
And the cattle munch content.

Dyfryg knew a good place when he found it.,
His pupils learned their lessons well.
They took his insights widespread in the land
And left their mark.

When will these humans learn to change their ways,
Despoiling that that nurtures all they have.
Obsessed by their own power, they do not see
The damage wrecked by arrogant narcissism.

Do they think I do not care?
Do they think I am inert?
Do they not understand
That the power who created them
Has an equal power to destroy?

[78]

Stained glass windows

A torrent, a cascade of tiny, jewel bright fragments,
Intensely glowing with the beauty of the earth,
The incandescent radiance of God.

The colours catch my breath,
The light pierces my soul,
I struggle with tears.

This is our world,
Appearing so solid and functional,
But composed of infinite, elusive, shape-changing particles,
Coming and going, not here, not there,
Beyond our grasp, teasing our comprehension,
Yet still our familiar home.

This man, this artist, he had understood.

[79]

Change

I have watched the world become richer - and poorer.

Richer in wealth - but poorer in courtesy.
Richer in things - but poorer in values.
Richer in style - but poorer in substance.

Richer in variety - but poorer in meaning.
Richer in know-how - but poorer in care.
Richer in fantasy - but poorer in rootedness.

Richer in choice - but poorer in discrimination.
Richer in fun - but poorer in satisfaction.
Richer in communication - but poorer in intimacy.
Richer in diversity - but poorer in culture.

I have watched the limits expand, the boundaries dissolve,
The colours ever brighter, all faster and faster.
Then a mad final swirl into a muddy brown.
No rainbow world this, but a murky mess.

A tired old woman, my vision is clear,
My illusions stripped, my own agenda done.
Change is a part of life, inexorable, inevitable,
But which way, at what pace, and how?

We need something old, we need something new.
We need to acknowledge who and what we are,
The basic needs of our incarnation,
Our utter dependence on the natural world,
Ourselves as a part of an ongoing creation,
More strange, more beautiful, more terrifying
Than ever we can comprehend.

We need humility.
We need the Light to enter our souls.

[80]

Healing

The scent of wet earth is a healing thing.
The burble of mountain stream over rocks is a healing thing.
To watch the fluffy white clouds on a summer's day is a healing thing.

The delicate wet-nose kiss of a small dog is a healing thing.
The weight of a baby's head in the crook of one's arm is a healing thing.
The stroking of a baby's hair, a dog's soft ear, is a healing thing.

A phone call from an absent friend - a birthday remembered - is a healing thing.
The boneless relaxation of a post-coital doze is a healing thing.
The sleepy holding of hands in the wee small hours is a healing thing.

The orderly home is a healing thing.
The silence of a Quaker Meeting is a healing thing.
To feel truly loved is a healing thing.

Why then do we fight?

[81]

Hymn

Sun on my face, soft breeze in my hair, I chat idly to my
 lover,
Watch the soft summer clouds drift across the clear blue sky.

The distant rhythmic roar of the outgoing tide
Is the heartbeat of this landscape.
A ground bass to the fluttering descant of children's chatter,
The piercing flute of swooping gull.

This earth is a beautiful place,
Always in motion, sustaining our life.

I sink into its deep stillness.

[82]

Epilogue

Dorothy

I entered your house
With reverence and trepidation,
Hoping to encounter your ghost,
But you were not there.

Your furnishings,
Imbued with warmth and welcome,
Looked old and tired.
Battered beyond repair.

A few good pieces,
But out of fashion,
And not my style.

Your bric-a-brac
Drenched in meaning for you,
Treasured, holding your history,
Devoid of significance now.

I miss your conversation and wit,
The shared and different experience,
The books passed to and fro,
The shared journey into dotage
And decrepitude.

I miss your confirmation of myself
As interesting, of value.
The exchange of viewpoints,
What we miss, and what deplore.

Above all I miss
Your utter coruscating intelligence,
And insight - and love.
There can be no other to compare.
RIP.

[83]

Gifts

A shower of gold highlights the hedgerows and the trees,
The verges are lit up as if by sunlight.
A gift of autumn come to gladden our hearts.

In my youth I was always searching for some such gift -
A drift of spring-time daffodils in the park;
A small and pretty Palladian gate-house;
A suburban garden bursting with bright flowers;
A plain severe facade of Georgian build
Amongst the fussy shapeless stretches of Victorian stuff.

Later, the rummaging in junk shops for our small first home,
The nerve of bidding at the local auction rooms,
The exercising of skill, a discerning eye
For something different, something interesting
Among the dusty detritus of others' lives.

Then, at the lowest of low ebbs
The arrival of our daughter safe and sound.
A perfect beautiful child who filled my world,
Who needed what I had to give,
And responded with delight.

Now, in old age, there is so much loss,
So much suffering in the wider world,
So much learned but lacking influence,
The misery can no longer be soothed away.
I have to acknowledge how it was,
Unbearable, deadly, and unnecessary,
A toxic place, a toxic home,
No model, no support for what was to come.

Today I struggled to the super-market,
Glad to finally rest awhile in the car.
A man came by with trolley, shopping done;
An unexceptionable man,
Middle-aged, close-cropped and balding,
In the dreary t-shirt uniform of our time.

His small daughter sat aloft amongst the groceries
Engrossed in playing with something in her lap.
His bright-eyed son bounced alongside his Dad
Chatting to him, sharing a joke, enjoying the outing.
A happy, functioning family briefly glimpsed.

Two good things found in one day.
Hope is still around the corner
If I can only see.

[84]

Shifting Sands

Once there was a warm and gentle sea.
In the summer we lived the beach life,
Snacking our fill on the small shelled creatures living there,
Making mountains of their skeletal remains.

We splashed and played on the water's edge,
Made love with the small waves lapping our skin,
The silky sand shifting beneath us.

We too have built on shifting sand,
Of a very different kind.
Among the lies and obfuscations of dysfunctional kin,
Where was the bedrock,
Where the truth, the basic fundamental reality.

Gradually, painfully we found it.
Learned to protect that vital creative core
Of love,
From envious destructive attack.

Created something sound and ongoing,
In our young who managed to survive.

But it wasn't much fun.
And it has left me tired.

What has the human race
Done to itself!

[85]

Letting Go

On your last visit you looked beautiful.
I saw then the woman you might have been
And knew the end was near.

You wrote, a brief apology,
Another damned cold - and very tired.

I replied, with gossip,
With insightful, angry comments
On the days's news,
Intending stimulation and amusement.
Too clever by half!

Perhaps what you really needed
Was a metaphorical holding of hands,
The tale of my own near-death escape,
And that it was alright to go.

We wait now, coping as we best can.
I think you understand.
Apologies superfluous.
May God go with you.

[86]

Clouds

As my attachment to earth thins
I watch the sky ever more.

Today a brilliant cornflower blue
Paling to light turquoise.
Great puff balls of white cloud.

A few wisps travel fast
Blown by a lower wind.
Bizarre.

Ahead a dark patch from heaven to earth.
Somewhere a shower is falling.

At evening, the rose-tinted remnants of day.
Sunset outlines a brilliantly gilt-edged mass.
At times the welsh dragon
Breaths out his fiery breath from the west
Evoking warmth and sadness and hiraeth.

Above the clouds
Where the aeroplanes fly
The sun always shines.

Beyond that, black darkness,
Aeons of space,
Terrifying emptiness.
But full of stardust
The matter of our creation.

Awe.

[87]

Notes

1

November 1979. The view from the kitchen living-room of my childhood home was of a two-storey high, red brick wall. I developed a fine discrimination of the many shades of brick!

2

December 1979

3

February 1980

4

June 1980.

5

Dog-walking from Weston was usually done alongside Bath racecourse at Lansdown. There is a lot of history in this area, including a very bloody Civil War battle. (Battle of Lansdown 1643.) Max, not usually an imaginative dog, once saw here a cobbly (a canine ghost), was scared rigid, and refused to cross an apparently empty stretch of grass. The next day he had forgotten his fear.

The sacred grove, a wooded knoll seen westwards across the valley, probably covers a neolithic or Iron Age burial mound. It can be seen against the skyline for many miles around, and probably marks the grave of a very important leader.

6

1980. For some years I travelled regularly between Bath and Nailsworth, acting as supervisor to a group of counsellors who subsequently became GCS - the Gloucestershire Counselling Service. This particular tree was a landmark on the journey. At this time, my husband had left academia to work in industry, and was frequently abroad. Neither of us much enjoyed the separations.

7

March 1982

8

December 1985

137

9
June 1995

10
October 1979

11
July 1980. A tribute to my analyst!

12
October 1980. My first visits to the Lake District were as a teenager, youth-hostelling, There was then a gap of many years before this next visit. One of my most beloved landscapes, we subsequently acquired a timeshare there.

13
July1982

14
1985. Alan was a friend of my adolescence, one of a group united by our intellectual pretensions, and a love of classical music. We tended to meet at concerts, in the municipal library on Saturday mornings, at the Kardomah for coffee if funds ran to it, and at each other's homes, listening to gramophone records.
Alan and I were very comfortable together, but his fearsome dragon of a mother made it almost inevitable that he would eventually opt for a gay life-style. It was he who introduced me to my future husband - and rather regretted it.
The landscape was the extensive tip of a worked-out coal mine close to my family's allotment on Mapperley Plain. There was some vegetation beginning to grow on it, but it was of a most peculiar and distorted kind.
I was recalling some afternoons spent here in our sixth-form years, when life felt very stressful but there was the promise of university ahead.

15
William Richard Orlando Gosling (Dickon) (1956-58) — a drowning.

16
December 1988. The cause of my anger was a period of time within my professional institution when a group of fundamentalists attempted a political takeover bid. As with all fundamentalist groups, it was impossible to have a dialogue, since there was only one possible perspective - theirs. As this attitude had powerful childhood resonances, I did not react kindly to it, and finally adopted my characteristic defence of withdrawal from the fray.

17
June 1995.

18
March 2003.

19
August 1979

20
February 2009. For another perspective on the same sub-culture, see the book or film of Alan Sillitoe's *Saturday Night & Sunday Morning*.

21
April 1980.

22
August 1980. Recalling a visit of my parents-in-law to our house in Weston, Bath.

23
Harry Ingle (Lal) (1908 – 1980) My mother's resident lover, and the third person in my childhood *menage à trois*.

24
February 1982. The second stanza would have been Lal's own reaction to death. He had no belief in an afterlife.

25
September 1981. Gwladys Mai Best *née* Evans (1905-2003)

26
December 2004. Melanie Susan Edwards *née* Gosling (1954-2004). Melanie was apparently fit and healthy until June 2004, when a diagnosis was made of colon cancer. She died in October 2004, having been nursed at her brother Ceri's home by her sister-in-law Vinny.

27
December 2004.

28
December 2004.

29
March 2005.

30
March 2009. For our first few months in Swansea in 1958, we rented The Watch House on Pennard West Cliff. Our next door neighbour happened to be Vernon Watkins, the poet and close friend of Dylan Thomas. We found him a reserved, kindly, deeply courteous man, and his tart comment surprised us. *Leftover Life to Kill* was the title of Caitlin Thomas' memoir, written after her husband's death.

31
April 2009. During a visit to Seville in March 2005, I had a brief, totally unexpected but powerful sense of Melanie's presence. With it came a rush of insight into aspects of her life which had hitherto been puzzling. There is an Iberian strain in the family's genetic inheritance which was very apparent in Melanie.

32
November 2008.

33
1993. In the 18th and 19th centuries, Swansea was the copper capital of the world, and was known as 'Copperopolis'. Copper ore was imported from far overseas, local coal was used to smelt it, and the exported processed metal constituted about 60% of the world's consumption. It was the world's first globally integrated heavy industry. During that period, the Strand was a vital hub of maritime activity.

In time the industry declined, but the resulting toxicity left a vast area of the Lower Swansea Valley blighted and utterly uninhabitable. It was only in the 1960s that the local authority, aided by the university, began the mammoth task of returning that environment to normality. It is now difficult to see where it had all taken place.

At the time of writing, the Strand was still in a state of decay and dereliction, made worse by bomb damage experienced during the 1939-45 war. I passed through it *en route* between a car park and the shopping area of town. More recently the city has been undergoing re-development, and the area is revived once more.

34
April 1986.

35
April 1986.

36
December 2009.

37
August 1996. Cefn Bryn is the highest point on the Gower peninsula, and the summit offers magnificent views in all directions. The neolithic monument known locally as King Arthur's Stone or Maen Ceti is situated slightly to the north and below the summit. From there one has an impressive view across the salt marsh and the Loughor estuary towards Llanelli. The mutton from the local salt-grazed sheep is much prized, and cockle gathering is still a local industry.
A broad untended grassy pathway lies between Maen Ceti and the summit of the Bryn. There is a timeless quality about the landscape.

38
August 1995. 'Nessies' refers to the mythical Loch Ness monster and its reputed photograph.

39
September 2007. Swansea Bay

40
March 2009. An outing to Pennard. The magnolia is *magnolia campbellii*, (or possibly '*darjeeling*') a very large species only flowering after 20 years of age. There were two magnificent

specimens behind Clyne Castle, a university hall of residence where we lived from 1963-68. This particular tree stands in a garden at the corner of Mumbles Road and the Mayals.

41

March 2012. Written when granddaughter Poppy, aged 21, was out in Afghanistan with the Territorial Army as part of a helicopter support unit. We were all - appropriately - anxious for her safety.

Having myself lost one child to an accident, and another to premature death from cancer, it was not an easy time. She survived, and was subsequently awarded the Afghanistan Medal for her service.

42

December 2010. Written when my two younger granddaughters were on the cusp of leaving home.

43

July 2009. No.1 granddaughter Rebecca had just been awarded the degree of Doctor of Philosophy at Royal Holloway - a tremendous achievement in the face of enormous odds.

The young soldier in Afghanistan, 18 years old, was knifed by a 12-year old boy and sent home for two weeks on furlough. On his return he was blown up twice, had both legs amputated, and brought back to the UK for intensive care. His morale remained high, and the army were enormously supportive to him, arranging rehabilitation and further duty.

44

July 2009. The previous day, we had watched our no. 1 granddaughter Rebecca awarded. That same evening we learned that eight more soldiers had died that day in Afghanistan. Several were only eighteen years old, the rest in their twenties.

45

September 2009. Josh was a friend and Territorial Amy colleague of our no. 2 granddaughter, Poppy. At his request, she visited him several times while he was in treatment at the military hospital in Birmingham, and was impressed by the level of care and support he received. Subsequently, the Army found him an administrative post, and he married a young woman who already had small children. He did not keep up further contact.

46

April 2014. I find myself doing some unofficial counselling! Easter is a celebration of death and resurrection. Both aspects were active in this encounter. 'My favourite theologian' refers to the Anglican H. A. Williams, author of *The True Wildernes*

47

March 2013. A return to old haunts. Oxwich is one of the loveliest bays in Gower. A fellow lecturer at Swansea in civil engineering, John Sandover and his wife Ann were hospitable friends in our first years there. Ann's Christmas lunch - and the bumpy car journey in our little Standard 8 - finally precipitated the 2-week late arrival of John Ceri Fabian Gosling!

48

June 2014. Written with no. 3 granddaughter Nancy in mind! Growing up in inner-city Nottingham was one kind of experience. In the 1930s horses were still a routine part of urban life. The large Shires were owned by Shipstones Breweries and were used to pull the drays along Hyson Green to the brewery at Basford. Their dung was much prized by local gardeners for their small back yard plots.

The contrast with our life in old age in a Somerset village is marked.

49

A phrase, fashionable in Regency times, for a depressed mood. One symptom of the cadmium poisoning we suffered (see 'The Magic House' *v.i.*) was a highly disagreeable and atypical depression, which can be discerned in some of these poems. Since blue house dust alerted us to the source of the problem, it seemed an appropriate term to resurrect!

50
January 2011

51
December 2011. This bout of misery was the result of a release of cadmium into the bloodstream - an experience that was repeated many times as we battled with the results of chronic cadmium poisoning This was a particularly fierce and disturbing bout. However, while the condition was physiologically induced, understanding the psychodynamics revealed was very liberating.

52
August 2013. Prompted by a visit to our old friends J. & P. B. in Swansea. The other two children are the grandchildren of another long-standing friend B. P.W.

53
June 2014. A wry comment on some family dynamics which rattle down the generations! Denial has its place as a means of survival in a crisis situation. As a long-term strategy, it leaves others to carry the pain, limits one's capacity to grow from experience, and ultimately can have destructive consequences.

I had considerable affection for the individuals concerned - and not a little envy of their resilience in the face of life's blows - but came to realise that there was a cost that was paid by those around them.

54
June 2009. I am reminded of the Hindu four phases of human existence. After the third - the lengthy one of the householder - there comes a fourth, when the now elderly person relinquishes all their burdens and possessions, and goes walkabout. I suspect I have reached that stage!

55
May 2010. The death of our daughter Melanie in 2004 remained a source of pain.

56
March 2014.

57
January 2010. The previous owners of our house stripped some of the walls down to bare stone and failed to seal them. It was fashionable at the time, and intended to emphasise the age of the

house, built around 1400 AD. The resulting (blue-grey) dust made us increasingly ill until we decided to paint the exposed walls white to match the rest. (Our ancestors would have lime-washed them.) Our slow recovery from the apparently unrelated clutch of symptoms took several years. Given the geology of the area, we suspect the dust contained highly poisonous cadmium.

58
June 2009. Stanza 1: dim memories of lying in the pram.

Stanza 2: In my childhood our annual family holiday was taken on the east coast near Skegness at Chapel St. Leonard's. A bracing (chill!) wind off the North Sea was a constant. Living in a soft coal area resulted in most children I knew having chronic catarrh and runny noses.

Stanza 3: The woodland grove was Lambley Dumbles, a favourite place for a weekend ramble. Clifton Grove alongside the river Trent was another favourite walk. Both places had an aura of ancient magic for me, and an exciting smell. Sadly, the latter has now been built upon.

Stanza 4: I have always found second-hand bookshops the most exciting places - irresistible! Music was a world where feelings could be safely located and experienced - vitally important. Whatever happened to the cultural pretensions of the BBC? The Home Service did a wonderful job at that time because it was the equivalent of today's Radio 4 and what most people listened to. Today's Radio 3 does not substitute! To be fair, Classic FM has done a great service in popularising classical music, (an independent initiative) but both these channels had to be FOUND.

Stanza 5: A kindly schoolteacher and her trainee Congregationalist minister husband, plus a colleague, took a gaggle of sixth-formers youth-hostelling in the Lake District. The landscape was a revelation; this first extended period away from home and parents a significant experience. We made a 12-day circular hike from Ullswater around to Wastwater and Eskdale, and climbed Scafell Pike in a heatwave! It remains for me a magical landscape.

59
April 2009.

60
July 2012. Childhood revisited.

61
September 2012. An amusing bit of social chit-chat at William's 80th birthday lunch at The Mill in Rode. It left me cogitating.

62
November 2010. A happy love-making

63
September 2013. Written for William on his birthday. He took it very well! The phrase 'robust idiotic optimism' was coined by one of Napoleon's generals to describe their Peninsula War adversary who refused to cut and run: the Duke of Wellington, another dyslexic.

64
September 2013

65
March 2011. This poem records an incident at a conference (Trialogue, March 2011) which caused me more irritation than it deserved. After some thought, the reasons became obvious to me. It was a replay of an all-too-familiar scenario, and one in which I can very easily get trapped. There have been a succession of such people in my life - some within the family - and I have been slow to realise that I have been seeking for a kind of mutuality which never develops. That is not the game that the other is playing! It has left me with a sense of having been exploited - of time and caring having been poured through a sieve! At the risk of rudeness, I simply cannot collude any longer.

66
January 2013. A poem prompted by the death of my friend Ann. The royal tearaway is Prince Harry; the young soldier our no. 2 granddaughter Poppy. The small boy in the photograph is the first grandson of Sandra and Trevor Cook. Trevor was once our Rector in Rode.

67
January 2013. Ann and I had been friends since we were 12 years old, when she was evacuated to my home town during the 1939-45 war. As a southerner, she already had a sophistication I

admired! Subsequently we both studied medicine in London, she at Charing Cross, myself at the Royal Free. She married a fellow medical student, had two sons - her mother sharing their care - but finally qualified, and went on to practise as a GP.

William and I spent the first year or so of our life together in one of several rented rooms in her house overlooking Hampstead Heath. By the time we left, we had acquired a small dog and a baby!

Ann subsequently left her sons' father and formed a happy and enduring relationship with an old friend. Later, for several years during my psychotherapy training, she provided me with a weekly bed for the night. That safe place was enormously helpful. She was a very good friend. Nontheless, she had a deep reserve which I never quite penetrated - and I regretted it.

68
April 2013. Mary was an active member of the Bradford-on-Avon Quaker Meeting, and still apparently in good health and involved with the community. She was found dead in her bed having taken steps to end her life. She left a carefully worded and loving letter which attempted to mitigate the pain for those left behind. The event was shocking for her fellow Quakers, and difficult for some to accept.

69
July 2013. Written following a visit from my old and dearest friend from schooldays. Our relationship has endured across the years and the continents. We are unlikely to meet up again.

70
June 2011. Kathryn (*née* Evans) was the daughter of my mother's brother Joe, and her family lived nearby. Eighteen months younger than myself and another only child, she too won a place at the local grammar school. We were not particularly close as children, but became much more so in our student and young married days in London.

The elder of her two daughters was born with several physical handicaps, and today would probably be diagnosed as mildly autistic. After some years the stresses within the family led to the breakdown of Kathryn's marriage, and some estrangement from her younger daughter.

When the older girl could no longer cope with caring for her 8-year old son, his grandmother took him to live with her in her elegant but small flat, sought help for his congenital heart condition, and supported his education through to university level.

71
December 2013. A celebration of Werner Othold's birthday - his 60th. We had been included in this annual family gathering for several years, and much appreciated being asked.

72
May 2009. Written for my daughter-in-law Vinny - with compassion! The granddaughter sharing Nana Gosling's kitchen was Nina Punt.

73
November 2012. I was on my way to my first cataract operation at The Circle Hospital near Bath, trying not to be anxious! The term 'squiggle' is a reference to the Squiggle game created by D. W. Winnicott, paediatrician and psychoanalyst *extraordinaire*, in his work with children.

74
Christmas 2010. In my perspective, all myths have a basis in reality, and all miracles have a naturalistic explanation.

It has been suggested that Jesus was the son of Herod Antipater, Herod the Great's eldest son, who was executed in 4 BC at Rome. If so, this would explain the Massacre of the Innocents at the time of Jesus' birth, the Flight into Egypt, and the later Crucifixion. Jesus would have been seen as a political threat to those in power.

75
May 2013

76
June 2009

77
September 2012. My friend, Patricia Turner, and I paid a visit to Hereford cathedral specifically to see this famous artefact. It was an interesting experience, and the accompanying exhibition was well conceived and informative. The deep sense of tranquillity

throughout the cathedral was moving, as was the exemplary quality of custodial care.

The large collection of books in the chained library suggests that Hereford was fortunate in avoiding much of the mayhem of life in other areas of the country, although there were times when it was drawn into the prevalent social disorder of the Border country.

78
September 2012. Written after a visit to the church of St. Dubricius (Dyfryg) in Hentland, Herefordshire. Dyfrig (c.465 – c. 550) was a towering figure amongst the early Celtic saints in Wales, and inspired and mentored an impressive clutch of younger men including Samson, Teilo and Illtyd. His large school and monastery was in this area of Ergyng. He was the major evangelist of south-east Wales, and also has a church dedicated to him in Porlock, Somerset.

79
September 2012. Written following a visit to Hereford cathedral where there is clearly a tradition of interest in the visual arts. There are some lively artefacts which link back to the mediaeval love of colour, as exemplified by the polychromatic paint on the tombstone of a knight and his lady.

In a small room are four stained glass windows, made recently by Tom Denny, which I and my companion found immensely moving.

80
August 2010. A comment on our perverse society. First published in *The Friend*.

81
July 2012

82
August 2009

83
August, 2016   Dr. Dorothy Speed was a remarkable woman — a highly intelligent medical practitioner who had a distinguished career in a number of spheres.

In her retirement she became a neighbour, and we developed a friendship that was lively and deep, such as one rarely forms in old age. She has been much missed.

Thanks to the kindness of her executor, Venetia Porter, I managed to rescue Dorothy's desk chair, a comfortable 18th century armchair which sits happily alongside my bureau of the same date. I treasure it, and the memories it brings.

84
November 2014
A low ebb!

85
June 2016 The beach life refers to our pre-historic past which has left great mounds of mollusc shells for archaeologists to find. Our cultural addiction to summer holidays at the seaside is, I suspect, a lingering tribal memory of that time.

86
February 2018. J. has been a friend and neighbour for 30 years, and we have lived alongside each other through turbulent times. She now has terminal cancer, but is living longer and more actively than anticipated.

87
May 2016. A brush with the numinous.

Patricia Gosling is of Welsh descent.
Growing up in Nottingham,
then a medical student in London,
she has since lived in
Swansea and the West country.

For twenty-five years she was in private practice as
a psychoanalytical psychotherapist in the gaps
between her primary roles as wife and mother.

Writing poetry was an unexpected
and very private activity acquired in middle age.

Patricia has been a Member of the Religious
Society of Friends (Quakers) for half a century

See also:
https://sites.google.com/site/pmgwritings/

As is usual in collected writings, some of the
poems have appeared before, notably in *Loving
and Loss* and *Enduring.*

Made in the USA
Columbia, SC
02 April 2018